LINKLOVE

With kind wishes

[signature]

Linklove

BARRIE WADE

HARRY CHAMBERS/PETERLOO POETS

First published in 1985
by Harry Chambers/Peterloo Poets
Treovis Farm Cottage, Upton Cross, Liskeard, Cornwall PL14 5BQ

ISBN 0 905291 70 0

Printed in Great Britain by
Latimer Trend & Company Ltd, Plymouth

ACKNOWLEDGEMENTS are due to the anthologies *Lines And Levels* (Lincolnshire Association for The Arts, 1972) and *Not For Ambition Or Bread* (Lincolnshire Association for The Arts, 1973), and to the magazines *Envoi* and *Poetry Matters*.

A version of 'Snowfields' was first broadcast on the BBC programme *The Northern Drift*.

'At Stud' was a prizewinning poem in The National Poetry Competition, 1981.

'Trophy' was a prizewinning poem in The National Poetry Competition, 1984.

Cover illustration: 'Compendium of Medicinal Plants: Picking Cherries'. (Sloane MS 4016 folio 30). Courtesy of The British Library.

Contents

	page
Linklove	9
Trophy	10
Devil Birds	11
Heron	12
The Watchers	13
Repossession	14
Dragons	15
Marsh Farm	16
At Stud	17
Snowfields	18
Dual Carriageway	19
Approach Road	20
Silent Rivers Run	22
Down to Earth	23
Towerblock	24
Reflections	25
Mixed Farm	26
Brightside	28
Perceptions	30
Nonspeaking Part	31
Linkstreets	32
Mine For Life	33
Ironbridge	35
Enemy Burial, Cannock Chase	36
Robins	38
Bluetit	39
Nuthatch	40
Magpies	41
Syntactic Structures	42
Between Tall Buildings	43
Conference	44
Severely Subnormal	45
Daffodils	46
Our Lady	47
Cat and Mouse	48
New World	50
Pictures of Woman	51
Poem for a Child	52

Linklove

You bring me cherries in a paper bag,
their juices pressed into a crimson blush
of skin, their tenderness of eyes that beg
the touch from me upon a cheek's cool flesh,

and down my years you tumble. I take
you to the teatable, the blacklead grate,
the seconds china Dad got cheap from Stoke
and little stones in tandem round a plate;

to Mum, with TB fastening in her cheeks
and cherry rubies dangling at her ears,
doing her gypsy dance . . .
                    . . .the breeze here seeks
from slanting meadow grass a dry applause.

Distance-drained to formal white and black,
a magpie stabs its stark routine at vision's edge
and some staccato elemental beat
rivets your presence to my past. The bridge

heaves and settles, linked loves hold the strain;
promises of youth renew in taste
and touch; remembered juices stream
to refresh our places parched by pain and waste.

Trophy

Your silver trophy haggards up my face
like shrinking mirrors that I used to hate
when Grandma took me to that seaside place.
Old shrieks, old gawpings menace in its plate.

My eyes reflecting in the polished curves,
rabbit-huge, distort between two withered ears.
The drawn skin ambers where a film of tarnish serves
to spread her marker over all the years.

The only cup I won was at the Grammar
sports for running miles on fifty fags a week.
That night I took it round to swank with Grandma,
smiling-sure her 'lazy sod' could stop her cheek.

But Gran had stopped herself. The gas pipe lay
beside her on the floor, pointing the dentured grin.
A fixed look bulged its poisoned rodent eye
and yellow tarnish stiffened puckers in her skin.

A rush of action followed then—the praise
of coroner, the prize of waking up
mature in people's looks. But now no pride allays
a terror that you bring me death inside a cup.

Devil Birds

Tempting a grounded swift to fly
the boy felt needle claws and fear
bite in his flesh, then into sky
launched a black flicker of knives. Each year

they dive from eggshell summer skies
with demon squeal and scream to wheel
and scribble speedpaths round the house.
Their evening is the slice of steel

and truly they become all blade:
scythes set slant upon torpedo backs
twist and flash in hurtling raid
after raid down the warm currents. Black

fork and crescent score their traces
into adult guts with surgings like desire.
Scimitar-hard, honed for slashes
at summer calm, the menace lasts, while higher

float the swifts to dark swallowings
at the edge of sight. There they take
their rest and pleasure on slick wings
blind to any human passion forced awake.

Heron

Air is not his element
Where he looks obsolete
Like some old transport—
Ponderous freight carrier—
A Hercules that cannot
Raise its undercarriage.

The reeds and shallows
Are his milieu
Where he proceeds by stealth.
His patience is supreme.
He can stay hunched
An age, dead as a post.

But his strike is snakespeed
And never seems to miss.
The jab is swift and lethal.
He will pickaxe rats
Or grapple fish
In a second's wink.

Will strip your goldfish pond
With head plumes waving
Over whiplash curves.
But knows his place. Is content
To earn his pleasure nonchalantly
With one foot on the ground.

The Watchers

In summer you may sense them on a wood walk,
Watchers with wary hearts pattering their breasts;
Yet their departing clatter triggers shock
Like long-awaited death after illness.

The fall of this one found a cradling hearse
Where birchtwigs in a mesh have grown.
Damp winter air seeps through its stiffening claws.

A lucky stone shot brings it thumping down.

A limp neck's rubbery loll and small head's
Swing hardly typify crop-ravager and pest.
The softest tints of rose and mauve instead
Salve and pacify the shot holes in its breast.

My fingers fan one slate-brown, step-tiled wing,
Its white expanded like a lily petal
Dropped on a corpse. The blood warmth seeks to cling,
Although its beak glints cold as cartridge metal.

Only after I have scraped a hollow,
Placed the bird and spread some leafmould over,
Explodes the sense of other eyes that follow
My ritual, eyes where blood throbs, eyes not filmed over.

I pass them lurking where the wood ends
Scanning the dusk, gun barrels bright as bone.
The fading death warmth startles in my hands
As the last fast fliers hurtle home.

Repossession

At dusk the old cathedral blackens
in steel sky, the teeming human flow
of workers drains to towerblocks
and metal chill of Autumn fastens
on an emptied city's concrete heart.

Walking separate we flinch in cold and quiet,
unready for electric sudden dins
of starling clouds that scream like drills,
wheel, settle and fill the few
cathedral trees with wingbeat mills.

Crude squabbles rasp the evening quiet
and our detachment. Cacophony shrills.
Trees billow and seethe. Fragments shake and splinter
off, flicker and merge again, bird and leaf
becoming indistinguishable.

The territorial chiding raid
goes out with light. Night ends the squall
with footholds on live trench-posts blindly gripped.
At dawn their droppings will lie spread
like bullets spent in massive war.

Our night patrol steps watchful, tense,
Craving in no man's land the dawn
attack, an armoured column's force
to crush the ghosts of germinating corn
and seed of poppies swelling before rain.

Dragons

The city's rebuilt heart seems ripe for shattering,
a brittle newly toughened zone hard
as jade, its flaws congealed with ancient blood
are overlaid by wide new spangled arteries.

With our windscreens we understand a sharp central
knock shatters the whole to crystals. Tension
loads each street and stress lines nerve
concrete with fissure networks blind and invisible.

The Chinese look for dragons underground
to blend their buildings with the dragon lines cast
in ridge and gully at the surface crust.
We merely punch old centres out,

unable to accept obscurity. The act
starts spider lines of fracture where
new angles seem unable to bear strain.
Sectioned towerblocks, raw offices, are stacked

cardlike for collapse. Maisonettes
missing the lapidary's art groan at their joints.
We do not bother over much. Separate,
segmented, we drive enshelled

through concrete channels whose streetlights
jewel our windscreens. We expect
to reach home without fuss, intact,
and careless about disturbing dragons.

Marsh Farm

Jem Pinney works this field by day
doggedly as ever, tightened
knuckles clipped around the tractor
wheel and jaw set by arid years
of treading muckclogged boots in sour land.

Time has dried curses in his throat
like thin winter grasses: Jem kicks
the dust from thistles with hopeless force
or as the wind in spasms plucks
at rusted spines of wire along the fence.

No wind snags in harsh wire this night;
baleful water on dull soil glints
uglyeyed, coarsened by moonlight,
and Jem's potato clamp lies blunt
and tensioned, rigid as a submarine.

Beyond the severed hands of elms,
where amber cords of highway thread
a sparkling town to dockyard cranes,
the level estuary gleams
and a smooth grace of carlights sweeps inland

where elegant refineries ride
like anchored pleasure ships, serene
and brilliant. Jem wisely works
his field by day: at night the calm
vast beauty all around would crack his heart.

At Stud

He tramples over metal churnings,
The man who makes machines.
His tackle of winches, jigs and clamps,
The scream of yielding steel proclaim him King.

His skill is seminal,
A learned judgment of hand and eye
For piercing holes in casings,
Each orifice true to a thou.

Fashioning machinery for him
Is important as birth. His mastery
Is fulcrum for fine grinding, milling of parts,
The true meshing of gears through life.

He prepares lovingly.
Alignment is made precisely accurate
And lubrication is exact
For routine spasms of probe and plunge.

His thick drill strikes through howling steel.
Squirming coils spill briefly down.
The shrill note changes
As the heated bit jerks in air.

He fills a wall with rows of precast Playboy nudes
Whose tungsten eyes approve his status.
Hack managers defer to him.
His ardour rings with profit.

Coralled to the screw of factory use,
Seasoned to throb of lathe and lever,
He starts at janglings in the far-off hills
And is bemused by open pasture.

Snowfields

The frankness of this land is ominous
though after snow it spreads most virginal;
while crows which straddle in the crystal fields
emphasise its modest unprotectedness.

Last year the unproductive bordering elms were felled
and now, in easy, driftless squandering,
unhindered gusts send snowpuffs flittering
where pleached thornhedges once conserved the field

that now lies bare. Soon eager gales of March
will ravage unrestrained over newsown
ground; as easily as scattering snow, they'll whisk
soil and splitting seeds into road and ditch.

The bentarmed gulls, when once the wind has died
will hang above aborted fields, casual
epitomes of how each spring the land
is hauled up by its elbows to be crucified.

Dual Carriageway

On my morning run I saw him
Fresh-killed on the fast lane.
Returned from his night run to pierce
Commuter rapid fire,
One of us caught him.
It was hard to think
his raiding days were done.
A glance revealed him still total fox:
brush fluffed as if newly washed,
Orange body slack, half-draped
as though his life had gently gone
to sleep, not been exploded out.
I carried his unbroken picture to the City.

Since then he has shrunk, not moved.
Rot and the car-wake swill have worn him,
jettisoned like a deck-brush
beached against a breakwater.
Each day he surely wastes
as if ripped by crows
hobbling in the slower lane.
For them, he bears in no-man's land
Too much the mark of man;
For us he bears
Too much the mark of beast.
So he will briefly stay, arching
The tarmac into grass, though now
Without identity, except to me
And maybe also to his killer who,
Despite contrary evidence, like me
Prefers to take a picture with him
Still unbroken to the City.

Approach Road

Still this is kestrel land: hung
on embankment currents, turning
in the white morning above a
strum of tyres that insulates
commuters from a hawk's business, one waits
for the breakfast our passing delays.

Misunderstanding, you say, *I thought they*
would not touch carrion. The idea dismays
us, devalues sleek
speed, superb eye and power
dive, makes a stunning
plummet merely stylish.

Above our hightuned glossy
strings the pulse of wings is grossly
overpowered for ease of feeding
off metalled roads. Their beating
says nothing yet of change, retains
an elemental rhythm.

Foxes have learned scavenging
from suburb bins, are at ease
in Edgbaston renewing
links with gentry. Nights padding
lawn and tarmac echo days
of ritual chasing when the fox was host.

The foxes keep their precedent
of losing: those crushed on city roads
have smaller skulls by ten percent
than country foxes, have a twist
of arthritis in the spine,
have paid the price of change in pain.

For a kestrel dilutions
of change are hard to estimate,
are imperceptible. It's hard
to feel wingpower degenerate
or an eye jewel lose one carat until
the pure rhythmic swoop becomes a charade.

And we have never measured
by the droop of hawk
or by the bone of fox.
Rhythms of our commuting runs ensured
that we became old trusties: now
the sight of freedom baffles us.

Silent Rivers Run

Veining the land our silent rivers run:
gutters more than drains, and patient salves for all
the seeping sores a festering landscape holds.

Pus-charged and slow the rivers run
virulent within deserted, poisoned banks;
for even rats have crept to kindlier sewers.

The fish died long ago or they remain
cordoned in upstream pools; those swept below
are floating crowmeat where infection concentrates.

With cancers in their blood slow rivers run:
below tall weirs a corpuscular foam hangs
lacily on hawthorn leaves and where it hangs it sears;

below the withering foam slow, silent rivers run
blackblooded to infect the loving sea
with early doses of industrial syphilis.

22

Down to Earth

They brought him back to Brum for burial.
Neatly nailed in oak he made the trip
In style across the city
To his own suburban colony.

He had never been so still.
On the flux of motorways
He lived his life in transit
Gulping miles to urban solace.

Weekends found him, cursing Sunday drivers,
Locked in a metal chain
Strung out to some resort.
Country became a space between towns.

Coronary had to be quick
To catch him away from home
At the conclusion of a deal
Before commission could be paid.

His hearse glides in through cemetery gates.
Strange that without prior canvassing
He chose to risk his own disposal
To the clutch of unknown earth.

Towerblock

A merger of concrete and glass
to regular tombstone grey.
Slab in the sky by day.
Proportionate uniform mass.
Night punches separate cells
out in dark or light. Random
patterns change as every life
goes its way. Nothing reveals
the tongueless scream so well:
every shabby sour staircase,
littered landing, scribbled wall
throttled to one dull symmetry.
Discord threads through fractured lives
in a labyrinth: one man roams
the cage a room at night becomes.
Coughs, the cries of beaten wives
settle like dust on stairs. All
troubles are known not shared. Stress
burns its acid through a paper wall.
A child screams. Lavatories gush
and whine. Electricity hums
in fluorescent tubes. Lifts clank
all night. A braying ambulance comes
and goes. Briefly the severed dark
is scoured for elemental
hints of death or birth. On all
gradations last lights die. Awful
dawn blanks the block grey and monumental.

Reflections

Indiscriminate
with slow certainty
a dingy evening
fastens on the town;
blunting scattered spires,
draining shine from slate,
smudging the edge of
stone, the dusk smokes down.
Asphalt blackens, streets
swirl in gloom, a mean
litter of garage
posters flare livid
tangerine and garish
pink, startle and gash
a tired afternoon.

Beyond the town where
sheepwall templates trace
their hillslope patterns
intricate and fresh
as hawthorn filigree,
derisive gullies
full of twinkling snow
crack open humpy
moors while overhead,
in blatant parody,
one red sunset smear
grins in a faceless sky.

The streetlights bring relief:
more sensitive than stone
we cannot long endure
the lovely mockery.

Mixed Farm

Flame cloudbands, ribbed in levels
where the sun slipped under,
carcass a desert sky
as though some beast encountered there
its raw, colossal slaughtering.
Cows bob leisurely at grass,
their misty breaths erased by dark.
One already trundles stifflegged
to hawthorn shelter. Nothing else
stirs. Sheep in the next field settle
like collapsed bags. Only light
falters as the crimson spills away
and drained undercloud dulls like meat.

Enough dithering grey remains
to show a crumpled file of huts,
an orchard tanglegrown, broken
farm house roof, the gentle lines
of hayricks dwarfed against a brash,
stark, corrugated factory
now the farm's replacement heart.

Light fades on time's trite accidents.
Today the deaf sow trampled one
of her litter, chomped marble-eyed
all through its squealing common death,
and one ecstatic lamb bounced high
enough to drown bottled in a drinking trough.

These errors always happened but change,
like strangling, is slow, best seen
in white and crude fluorescent glare
from farm house windows that reveals
the farmer, isolated, bent
to calculations of the price
of feed and fertiliser, whose

sons have chosen other work,
whose life is ruled by market trends
he cannot now control, whose hands
on calculator buttons fix the choice
of cauliflowers or sugar beet.

He has not seen this poignant flare
and fade of beauty in his sky,
beset by acre-yield and subsidy
and moisture levels of his grain.
An instrument of distant managers, he feels
no wad of earth beneath his nails.
Soon he will not even notice rain.

Brightside

I take responsibility for waste
here in England's arse, under drystone-and-
dale land where sewage farms and tips
scatter amongst cruder factory filth.
From here to Attercliffe land flinches
from the vigorous clamp of iron.
Carbon crust on stone is testament
to heavy wielding of metal. Earth slumps
beneath the binding spokes of railway lines,
Chimneys jut and ram at sky
and nothing here is regular save studded
rivet rows and tilted cranes
and the blackness, matt and uniform, backed
by blacker furnace, mill and foundry-bay.

I grew away from these yet each return
forges a meaning from disordered elements.
The heaps of coal and earth and waste—
among which creeps a leaden Don—
reform and tinkle over weirs.
The ground of slag and ash compounded sees
me returned to finger at its crust,
boy again, compulsively scab-picking.

With each return decay is more advanced:
rot compacts rubble, metal flakes to rust;
in factory yards grow sapling sycamores
and on embankment sides lupin, dogrose
and meadowsweet affirm a curious
ancient eloquence. Bindweed speaks
through rubble, plumes of willowherb force stone
apart and lichen sets its tongue on steel.

And I think of Spender's Black Country, seen
by train, and its antithesis in verse—
his *language of flesh and flowers* that spoke
Creation to him in a mass of grey.

I do not crave that verbal salve
and can accept the simple crudity
of power's excrement. I can become
as inarticulate as chimney cowls:

dumb birds that hunch against the mottling wind
and look to Tinsley's curving cooling towers.

Perceptions

Sucked by the sun's scene painting
in leafdropping jonquil and tender green,
I come with crayon and water
colour, set an easel against
the spring wood's vision, missing
at first in a leafhung pause
the tramp, cramped, reptilian,
broken by age and shy of light,
shrunk in a little space of dark.
Since neither of us can give ground,
my brushes finger him out
in image onto cartridge paper.

Grinning gnome in a trimmed garden,
he stares now fixedly untrue
to the one imprinted message
we exchanged that now I cannot grasp
a flash of eyes timorous as fauns
darting away to thicker fronds.

Nonspeaking Part

Army boots clash across the cafeteria;
an English soldier brash with first rehearsal tension makes
the drained airport echo like an empty theatre.

One of the professionals, he vaunts at the bar
for the pale girl there, parades a slim repertoire
of swaggers, winks. She is no ingenue

yet will not be his Columbine. Thinlipped
and plain she steelyeyes him, blandly slops
his tea, rebuffs him for the Cause, gives me

warm, superfluous smiles. Poor buffoon, he knows
he's been outfaced, droops, then grips his rifle,
gulps his soured drink, sinks to low profile

by the wall as her silence bullets home. Irish
soft eyes meet mine with no coquettish
interest now the masks are changed. I feel

only the crying loss of person to a role:
after the bomb's crude climax hatred fragments fall
to be improvised and polished for performance.

Linkstreets

Just off the Crumlin Road gaps are plugged
With brick. Agnes Street still wears its shutters
With stiff decency like pressed steel dentures
And pennies placed in sockets of dead eyes.

Bombers scorched Northumberland Street
To silence, shrivelled talk to slogans
Forced inarticulate retreat
And behind boards nonpartisan rats worked on.

A few houses remain unblanked,
Rashly vulnerable in the charred terrace.
One is outspoken with geranium tongues
Jauntily live in a window mouth.

Emblems of death and life are mocking
Pictograms of Army jargon
Which calls these streets an interface.
Otherwise the talking here has stopped.

There are no words for a crouched soldier
Isolate in risk and readiness;
None for the woman left alive with flowers
Among other, blinded windows.

Her son was gunned in Roden Street.
A bullet blossomed redly in one eye
And stopped his talk. For her
His funeral garlands had no tongues.

The human gaps force terrace jaws apart.
Vengenace wedges in with pity's tongue.
Voices become strident across distance,
Are stiffly bounced from brick and steel.

Mine for Life

Give me Timothy Malone
Who shocked his gentle mother
When he started school.
Refusing sandals he demanded
Hardtoed shoes to kick
The Christian brothers with.
The child tries on his roles
As readily as shoes
And words divorced from feeling,
Words for nudging: *Think this way*,
Words to take sides with,
Shape the separate parts
A man might later play.

Or give Michelle O'Connor's friend
Who missed a bomb and playschool
By accident of birth,
The newborn child at home
A more attractive toy
That morning than Michelle
Who outside briefly
Flowered in a ball of flame,
Her father's hand on the ignition
Some safe bomber's detonator.
The friend may fashion from a mesh of words
How an infant's death may help a Cause
Or build a shrine of guilt to celebrate her.

Give me Brian McDermott's friends.
A shiny placard marks
His murder place
Across from Park Parade,
A public plea for eyes
To wince away from.
His friends have fully learned
Of death's indifference.

They know the killer of a child
Somewhere strolls free,
Perhaps plays Mahler
In a quiet room, makes silent
Sunday collections graciously.

Give me the boy who daubed
The crimson hand and *No Pope here*
On saint Augustine wall,
And the girl forced to kneel
While hooded boys startled out
Her father's life through bullet holes
Smaller than communion wafers.
His lessons have been overlearned
In the slogan's shrieking pattern
And rigid emblem's shrilling force;
Hers in the silent smell of blood
And ritual nonchalance of death;
Mine in vain searchings for remorse.

We taste the bile of city war.
Even the unborn clank in wombs
Waiting to learn the taciturnity
That comes with bearing loss and pain.
Ashes of guilt and bitterness
Smear the children's brows with trouble.
Tied to a self-destructive city's urge
They crave carbolic cleansing
And quiet climax of release
From toxic words and strutting signs.
But their rhythm is the sway and
Deadpan march of grim apprentices,
The steady locking up of minds.

Ironbridge

The bridge arcs a rainbow curve in even
tracery of metal rails rayed
level along its span where our footsteps
splatter their raindrops on iron.

Avoiding each other's too-bright sunstare
we share the valley's steep infolding shade;
silver-straight our gaze slants to the river
beneath, as if in detail we perceived

the waterspiders scudding their slick
slaloms. Lacking time and touch to bracket
true parabolas from me to you, we weld
with words alone our sundered fabric.

Since derelict days have left our content
ravined with gulch and gully, our lament
for symmetry is inarticulate.
Only as evening gloom begins to fill

the arch do eyes across our void make straight
links purer than even this lovely crescent.
To the limit of our legal time we seek to vault our gulf
With girders enough to make a slender structure permanent.

Enemy Burial, Cannock Chase

May sunshine fires gold on Douglas firs
among whose poles your childvoice rings
its play alarms. Cuckoos siren and a blaze
of swallows strafes through cobalt clearings.

So the cemetery folds us in surprise,
its grave platoons set in neater
rows than marching men. Your wide eyes
tally ranks of fieldgrey slabs. Your chatter

dies like silenced birdsong. Your hand
grips as I read names—Gunter, Klaus,
Jurgen, Wilhelm. You comprehend
reverence, not why countries clash.

Dead millions overspill your mind. I tell
then of the grandfather you never knew
gassed at the Somme with shrapnel
crowding an arm and froth his lungs,

a teenage wounded who came near
erasing son and captive grandchild
who settles printed on the forest air
lost to the fragrance of a Summer field.

When I walked Belsen camp a year ago
corpsecrowded mounds merely appalled
where horror was blown massive through
public obelisk and memorial wall.

Here the griefs are small and personal—fresh
flowers sent from German towns by terse
old men remembering a son's smash
from skies to lie under these conifers,

tired as though from *trimm dich* in a wood
near home. Their channelled grieving swells
beneath my talk of childhood
cellar nights inside a father's arms, spills

through remembered fires, reflected rocket flares
upon a bedroom wall. Words pass
on but sadness stays. Silent we watch where
butterflies stitch gravestones to the grass.

We feel the yearning love of thousands killed
swell at our throats, the hopes of fathers lost
in avenues of stone, crescendos of waste
clarion for you, for me, my child.

Robins

They materialise vivid as rainbows,
come to heel in the eye corners
drawn to the arc of human work.

Spade shuttling does not startle their imprinted
orange-red off neutral earth.
Head turn and tilt and round deep eye

thread something querulously imprecise
between the gardener and his swing
and loose bright ironies in air:

for we fashion emblems from implicit
trust that also smashes them,
poor innocents, on our machines;

these minions king their own domains,
while others cower in continental woods
and hug fear to them as a covenant.

Bluetit

Nomadic sprung-steel visitor,
dapper you come capped, in formal
tie and collared, oversmart
for the total circus you perform.

Your arcs trapeze our air, branch tips
dip their trampolines. You strongbeak
milktop metals off, can swarm string
and twist a somersault round twigs.

Your feeding is a marionette on strings.

Clown companies stage the social warmth
that we in double-glazed suburbia
have lost, re-enact in miniature
the tumbler troupes of our forgotten age.

And there are some that play
the acrobatic season, display
the butterfly float and rising flight
against our plum leaves, miming dragon-flies.

From these the ancient pump spouts
flowers of moss and woven hair
later to fountain cobalt
into early summer air.

Nuthatch

His eyemark suits a masquerade,
imparts a raffish elegance
to slatebacked uniformity.

He doubles as pale kingfisher,
shows outline of a woodpecker
to fool unwary audiences.

His voices too impersonate
tit and thrush; he can lumberjack
a hazel shell viced into bark.

Disguises fall like husk around
an essence poured in headlong walks
down tree trunk verticals

in which he is unique, recalled
to individuality
by motion fluid as a waterfall.

He mirrors social human worlds
where liquid self may shine, affirms
the crystal flow behind a mask.

Magpies

They break air singly.
Overruddered glides
broomstick pallid skies,
dagger beak and cloak
trimmed for the hacking
robbing trade that is
their black business.

But mugging's not their style—
hardly suits the glossy flaunt,
their jaunts on sheepback
and white flashing of parts.

Each blatant couple
struts a hedgerow beat,
strips out egg and chick,
acknowledges alarm
cries like applause
with sideways hop and fleer.

Their cackles deflect sin
and nestling deaths are swaggered off;
their maggot jabs through cowpats light
no cauldrons of disgust.

Man is their only scourge.
He tallies them tattered
like washing on a wire.
An iridescence fades
and they hang nondescript:
drowned old women
tied to ducking stools,
the curses bottled in their breasts.

Syntactic Structures

Lena came for another trip tonight (it will
be the last, she knows) and afterwards in bright tones
at the door, 'Goodbye,' she said, 'and thanks for
having me.' My sensibility stirred its bones.

Of course it was too late to start again at depth:
preprogrammed as we were to surface cues,
it suited better to accept for supermarket wit
that Lena knew she had been had—was glad of it.

I did not answer, did not check her progress through
the garish lamplight into tunneled dark;
habit decreed my stimulus prompted her response
and so she went, treading the echoes of that one remark.

That I should map relationships between an echo
and what I feel she felt is patent irony:
that remains a way I had not sought to enter
her. When now each insight lights a different centre

the abstract relations remain unsolved
and another cheerful robot claims
an automatic translator's place
at communication's most mechanistic interface.

The wirebasket world preserves inside
(and most successfully) its showbiz talk
or journalese. We made the mesh too wide
and what slipped through was generative.

One begins by knowing what is lost—or never
did exist. Lena and I intuitively grasp
when love or language cannot be renewed
the primary defence of ambiguity.

Between Tall Buildings

Between tall buildings kamikhaze snow-
streaks harry into ground,
jet down my window where the eye fails
in separating objects
from trajectories of crisscrossed lines;
speedpaths framed by glass and steel
catch a moment's elegance before
extinction, liquid below.

I watch others shower
in deep central spaces and, trapped
by turbulence, hang, drift
and waver, tentative as changing minds.
And some there are
which at the currents' vortex act
like midge-clouds pencilling
the air and seeming not to fall, clusters
spiralling always up,
dancing their separate dogfight zigzags
in tight control of gnat or tigermoth.

Thinking etches you
against the Imperial lid of sky;
I also race and plunge,
tilt and climb. Your delicacy sings me
upward. Eventually
I may self-destruct, but for the moment I
soar between tall buildings.

Conference

A mild inconvenience: waking
at five to damp September
ninety miles from home; taking

the tight walk down college lino (Cambridge
girls were not expected to be taken
short) is mere discomfort. Swollen

guts swash with real ale and wine;
Knocking heart and velvet tongue remain,
as residue of discourse. Then

straddling the bowl I affront
exclusive dignities of brass
handles, the decent magnolia gloss.

Meanwhile despairing you were seeking
out my room bringing heavy metal
of your failing marriage for off-loading.

Breakfast finds you tranquillised
numb and confiding, the chance for comfort
gone; now my watchful joking shunts

your burden back to settle as a smudge
of drizzle round the cherry trees
gauzing your pain's bright unrelief.

Eventually a shame blows through our mesh
of words. The leaden morning makes us wary
of becoming inconvenient. Our search
is for excuses to avoid the final plenary.

Severely Subnormal

Fishlike
Her finger darts
And jabs to trace her name.

Eyes bob at letter rocks
And startle off.
The task

Ripples her forehead
Over fronds
And lengthening shadows of her brain.

We cannot grapple her.
Only the stagnant urine stink
Connects us lovingly.

Her salamander
Tongue lolls
Its semicaverned lizardry.

Sluiced from fissures
In her mind
Spittle rivers slob and bubble over it.

We are out of depth,
Angling
Concepts of self

To help haul
Her jelly body
Through the gape of time.

Daffodils

Travelling north together before (just)
you were a friend, I told in eulogies
of daffodils I'd seen before, soldiers
parading under city walls, jonquil dressed

for ceremony. You expressed regret
since your home garden held them greensheathed still
and so far north Spring slowly splits the shell
of earth. That sense prevailed and we forgot

until the cry of pleasure when you saw
them first. Ambered by headlights, their dazzling
splash of mellow gold sent April rippling
through our ordered year, yet I was slow

to articulate its message clarion.
Rooted in you now I share their silent
strain

   mute trumpets voiceless to prevent
an early velvet flowering smash violent
on barricades of long-established, public stone.

Our Lady

Child, your clear eye fixes on the gaps
and rightly. In your scan are demons,
trefoiled arches, angels and kings,
martyrs and the endless virgins
of the iconographers' bible;
yet the bald tormentings of hell
leave you unmoved. Toad and reptile,
fantasy of chimaera, ghoul and gargoyle
hunched in stone you tally
without words. Your appraisal
of tympanum and gallery
is so even-eyed that anguish
startling the narrow street seems
to spring from somewhere else, a mockery
perhaps of quarried face or scream
frozen in granite. Swelling again
your live cry rasps the stones. Your pain
draws glances. Your stare enters a portal
where the virgin suave with nonchalance
looks past you, miming her child's presence
in a permanence of cradling arms.
You sense the rending of stone.
Your cry recalls the snatch
of Christchild rooted from his worldly
mother whose eyes you cannot catch.
Your plastic features lend the grief
she has not shown through centuries.
My hand in yours is warming comfort.
I tell of 'naughty men' who smash
and steal, a truth that heals
your hurt for now. Crowding years soon
will teach of outrage and indifference,
the shattering of human mass and form.
Then I pray you will not also notice absence
grow hard inside you like a lapidary moon.

Cat and Mouse

In the shed a scrape
And scurry that can not
Be honeysuckle pattering outside.

Breaths are stilled, mine, yours and whatever
Scratched on the potfilled shelf.
Claws rattle on wood.

Your childblue eyes widen
For sight of hairy troll or dragon
Coils among the cobweb shreds.

A small hand creeps to mine.
Amplified in stillness, the dry
Clatter comes again.

A faint scritch and shriek.
A plummet drop to ground.
A twang elastic into garden tools

You squeal and start.
No fancied ghost or paper witch, but mouse
Enough to set hearts pounding.

We laugh to exorcise
The shame of fear. A mouse
Can bleed as no ghost can,

So excitement tingles on.
I even let you choose the mode
Of death. You lock

The cat in bristling
And, emperors for entertaining,
We peer at the window.

The show palls. She
Pads shelves fluidly then stares
Gladiatorial arrogance.

We weary of no action,
Forget and later release her catsprung
Steel by accident.

We find no body ripped,
No half-chewed rag of mouse,
Only a clawed

Pile of shavings and three inch-perfect
Infant mice cold dead, their button
Eyes skinned over.

If only she had chewed
Or maybe scratched them just a little. Inert
They excited no attention.

Perfect fleshpieces, emblems of unspoken guilt,
They stay to teach the truth of claws on wood,
Of death, cold at the heart of sport and fantasy.

New World

We who have briefly taken trips to ease
the urban walling-up have newly found
a continent (more precious than release)

in breakers headlight-silvered, pinewoods cold
at noon, have trod the ancient span of bridge,
church and city wall, as if seeking old

precedents for a bright love not looked-for.
Now, after sharing bodies' silks to tongue
and touch, more than ever I require,

when the city crawls alive, a lonely pathos
to recall green Gatsby visions of your promise—
and Dvorak's slow cor anglais sings me close.

Pictures of Woman

This Yankee winter sabres into bone,
hacks me to knife edges of sculptured bronze
past which your lovely essence beckons
through conditioned air. Three Europeans

spread you piecemeal. Vuillard patterns
you ordinary, shaped in lines
of tidy bed and yellow curtain
swept for access to a washing

bowl. Picasso splays you nude
and simultaneous, angling
in shallow space your fractured planes
that shift and net and show at once
both tilt and downpoint curvatures.

Then Miró makes your massive female dance
both brash and buoyant, girlish-crude
with paintbox colours paletted by lines
that trigger Tarragona where we walked once
in heat with little thought of Royo
dyeing fleece to tassel you this new.

The pictures wind your wholeness
from their European strand.
Three steps from reality makes
me still a mid-Atlantic man:
your patterns becoming facets, then random links;
your moist heat shuttling me stateless.

Poem for a Child

Child, you are quicksilver in talk
of elf and goblin that people
your world. Words spill and splash brilliance
while our prosaics fail to grasp
you. Protean in your elements,
You are all time shaped into flesh;
You fashion sand, water, stars and paint
to your own use, making the fresh
connections behind innocent
eyes where others cannot follow.

About your superiority Wordsworth was right.
We do not now respond to magic,
our glimpse of glory shrivelled in the light
of adult day and silver starpoints
starting even now to prick
the darkening fabric of the day
make us no important messages.

So we shall love you as our life's
star, more than a changing sky—
You tolerate our irritation,
our adult lack of attention—
and we must also love a cloud
we cannot hold, with selfless
love to let you separate,
reform and float away.